# ANTECHAMBER
## & OTHER POEMS

# MICHAEL McCLURE

# ANTECHAMBER
# & OTHER POEMS

A NEW DIRECTIONS BOOK

ACKNOWLEDGMENTS
Grateful acknowledgment is made to the editors and publishers of magazines, books, broadsides, and recordings where some of the material in this volume previously appeared: Archer Press (Oakland, Ca.), Arif Press (Berkeley, Ca.), *Atlantic Monthly, Beat Diary, Beatitude, California Living, Co-Evolution Quarterly,* Giorno Poetry Systems, *Kayak, New Directions in Prose and Poetry, New Poetry* (Australia), *Partisan Review, Rolling Stone, Roof, Truck, Unmuzzled Ox,* The Unspeakable Visions of the Individual (California, Pa.).

"The Mad Song" is from the play *The Grabbing of the Fairy,* which has been performed by the Company Theatre of Los Angeles, the Kitkitdizze Players, and the Magic Theatre of San Francisco. "Song from a Play" is also from *The Grabbing of the Fairy* and was included in the Magic Theatre production. Both poems are included in the limited edition of the play published by Truck Press (St. Paul, Minn.).

"Antechamber," section one, was originally published as a limited edition in 1977, designed by Maria Epes of the Poythress Press (Berkeley, Ca.).

The epigraph by Federico García Lorca is from "Gacela of Unforeseen Love," translated by W. S. Merwin and included in *The Selected Poems of Federico García Lorca* (Copyright © 1955 by New Directions Publishing Corporation).

First published as New Directions Paperbook 455 in 1978
Published simultaneously in Canada by McClelland & Stewart, Ltd.

Library of Congress Cataloging in Publication Data

McClure, Michael.
   Antechamber, and other poems.
   (A New Directions Book)
   I. Title.
PS3563.A262A8     811'5'4     77–25300
ISBN 0–8112–0682–3

New Directions Books are published for James Laughlin
by New Directions Publishing Corporation,
333 Sixth Avenue, New York 10014

"No one understood the perfume
of the dark magnolia of your womb.
No one knew that you tormented
a hummingbird of love between your teeth."
—Federico García Lorca

# THE RAINS OF FEBRUARY

THERE'S CRUELTY IN
EVERY JEWEL
and each black lump
of coal
was once a multitude
of lives.
Within his skin
each guru
holds a fool
but
none
like
me
who secretly contrives
a liberation
filled with buttercups
and blue-eyed grass
and golden tracks of spring
upon the hill
and air that's filled
with scent of rose
and dill.

# WATCHING THE VULTURE

*Drake's Bay*


I'M TOO CLEVER NOT TO GO ON LIVING!
BUT
the star bursts
from my brain
like a silver blaze
from a sun-struck wave.
I'M
TOO
SLY
not to know
that gliding vulture
is the flow
of the biomass
hurled out to feast
on the spreading yeast
of itself.
We are all incredible
sculptures of molecules!
I stand here like a raccoon
on the asphalt
hearing the voices of ravens
—and I blink in the sun.
This meal has just begun.

# BY THE HIGHWAY

*for Frank Ottiwell*

THE RACCOONS ARE WEIGHTLESS.
The burden
of the yellow glow
from the headlights
would weight them
to the ground
except
for the flow
of energy
in their legs
and black paws.
They almost
ignore us
from
their perfect
world
and
sniff
and
claw
at the galvanized
drainpipe,
shuffling to a nervous
and exultant measure.

3

# BORROWED FEET

LOVE ME FOR THE FOOL
I AM
(the laughing angel-imbecile).
The thrill
of kissing you
is seeing me
reflected in your eyes.
We try for purity
but
still
we're glorious
blobs
of meat.
I worship you
like blood
or oil or wheat.
Our love is flawed
and swallowed
by the rush of time.
A mindless innocence,
they say,
is crime.
We dance on borrowed feet.

# POLITICAL POEM

ANARCHY LEADS
to perfect discipline.
The sin
of Emptiness
is born of steady progress.
Let
us
laugh and scream
our way
to fine-edged embarrassment.
We're merry
hungry grizzly bears
within a tent
of gossamer.
We're balls of lint
upon a shining
floor.

---

The eyes of deer.
Black holes in space.
The look upon
a lover's face.

# THE LIST

—OLD MEN SLEEPING
IN SPEEDING CARS,
a hawk on a boulder
dripping with fog,
ten deer
in an autumn meadow,
yellow
aspens,
bishop pines
by the ocean.
These all speak more
as our stiff-
ness re-
laxes
into new birth.
The worth
of *things*
cracks open
and shows
the intestines.

———————

Glittering
gold
trembling
on darkness.

# WILDNESS

TRUE WILDNESS
IS COMPRISED
OF ACTS
that are not
domesticated.
See, the cloud
of repetitive
sex
is the despair
of the caged.
The adolescent strut
of grown men
is not free movement
but
the madness
of stress.
The endless murders
and soiled
bodies
are the mess
of robots
and social ogres.

WE
WHO
SEE
CLEARLY
APPRISE
YOU
OF THIS!

Oh, swim
in the world;

Liberty
can be unfurled.


# TO THE DRIVE-IN TELLER
# AT THE BANK


YOU FACE ME WITH
THE COLOR PHOTO
OF YOUR CHILD
taped to the window
as if she were you
and the universe
were some
mild
beast to smile on
the endless
reflections
of your image.

I hope you're right.

Our minds are daubed
with opalescent caves.

# FREEWHEELIN'S TATTOO

FRANK, HOW PLEASED
I AM
to see that Death's Head
tattoo of red and blue
blocked in
with solid black;
how good
to view the sign
of madcap finality
filled up
with darkness
to make a wing shape
forever flying
on your arm.
It
is
your new charm
or token
and it shows
that spirit cannot
be broken
but ever grows
toward flight.

# THE MAD SONG

*from a play*

ALL OF THE CREATURES AND ALL
OF THE FEATURES
stare back at here from somewhere else.
The blue and purple and golden seizures
have the odor of elbows when black sugar melts.

Then all of nothingness dives through space
and leaves fat care behind.
The innocence born on a face
is the substitute for mind.

The roses and oaks are okey doke.
The hills are beautiful pie.
Seriousness is the merriest joke.
Away, away, the boulders fly.

Lovers breathe with the breath of mint
and wc tickle our nose on the kitten's belly,
and we tickle our nose,
and we tickle our nose
on the kitten's belly.

# DESPAIR IN THE MORNING

THERE ARE VERY FEW IN SEARCH
OF THE DIVINE!
It is not crime or love
that intrigues us
for they are part
of the thrust
that
strives
and presses
in each conceivable
direction.
The dust
upon our feet
is galaxies.
Our lives
are a weird confection
created by the Social Ogre
that we are.
Everything
we
know
and
do
is a dissection
and plodding rearrangement,
and defamation,
of
our shapes
and our estrangements.

# POEM WITH A GIFT

OUR FACES IN OLD
MIRRORS
look no
younger
BUT
strength
lies
in the length
of wrinkles.

---

Knobcone pines.
Necks of tortoises.
Eternal deserts.
Pure nuggets.
The burls
of redwoods.
Polished roughness
of the walnut.

# LITTLE FANTASIES

WHAT ELEGANCE
TO BE A LIVING PEARL
in a clustered swirl
that spins through
time and space.

---

Throwing out
a lacy net
of loops
from
my
trajectory,
I
catch
this self
in momentary
immortality.
I'm Goethe,
Schiller,
or a white
white weasel
dashing on the snow.

# TWIN PEAKS

THE ORANGE FIRE OF SUNSET
BEHIND THE BLACKNESS
of the tree trunks
gleams
as a fireplace;
and the golden lace
of windows
ornaments the peaks.
On
the ocean
there's darkness
like frozen smoke
in lightless
universes.
Yet it's all
as gentle
as a baby's smile.
Sparrow hawks sleep
in the creaking
branches.

# EMILY DICKINSON'S HOUSE

*for Sam and Ann*

WITHOUT PROPERTY CAN WE
BE REAL?
How can we feel
the unknown facets
of ourselves
without a parcel
of hard property?
Look there's a tanager
and also indigo buntings
in the sunset!
Waterfalls
cataract
upon the mind.
See,
the star
that touches us
with hands of light.

The house we live in
is delight.

# IN A GUEST BOOK, N.Y.C.

CROCUSES AMID THE SNOW.
on Bank Street.
The Village buildings
move like a fleet
toward spring
and spread their shoulders
from the boulders
far below.
How
beautiful!

# POETICS

YES! THERE IS BUT ONE
POLITICS AND THAT
IS BIOLOGY.
BIOLOGY
IS
POLITICS.
We dive into
the black, black rainbow
of the end
unless we spend
our life and build love
in creation of
what is organic.
The old views
(worn and blasted)
are a structure
of death.
Our breath
IS
TO
SERVE
THE ULTIMATE
beauty
of ourselves.

# THE ENERGY AND CONSCIOUSNESS CONFERENCE

*Gainesville*


IF THE EYE MAKES STRUCTURES
WITH INHERENT
PATTERNS
then
we
are led
and built
by what
we see.
(( AS
someone
*else*
made
a frame
on
TV
or
film
to trap us,
trick us,
hold us
in
this
social strata )).

---

I WANT
LIB-

ER-
ATION!
I am a nation
of freed
slaves
and selves!


## ON  READING  PATERSON  ALOUD


YES,
THIS  IS
PURE
POETRY
—like Blake rambling in the fields
or snakes by the lakes
where we raise high the shields
with our names.
Man, city, waterfall,
are all the same.
This April book is free
of shame
and it dances
and glows
in the darkness
of a Past

that is not far away!

# THORNTON BEACH

WE ARE ENFOLDED, ENCASED
AND SELF-CREATED
IN A CRAZED
AND LOVELY
sea
of
Chaos
—and enwrapped
and untrapped
in the hand
that holds
the golden flower.
The body sups
on buttercups.
But
the waves!
keep us
raving
with their savory
thunder
and their roaring!

# BEGUN ON MOUNT TAMALPAIS

LIKE MOUNTAIN GOATS THAT MEDITATE
on Gods of Disappearances,
we watch our things
and smile
and clutch
at what the August brings.

Dry honey on the breeze,
and hummingbirds
above the chapparal,
and ivory towers
sprouting from the city frieze
are empty zeros
locked within the trunk
we fill with implements
to tease
the shape of thoughts.

Our lives
are grottoes
that we seize
with empty hands
away
from tongues
of moths.

# AT THE STEELE RANCH

I HATE THE BARE FIELDS!
And those who made them!
Their contempt
for diversity
breeds
hotter life
in we
who care.
The barn owls swoop
to look at us.
The hummingbird
sips
nasturtium nectar
from a grinning
flower.
Wings and faces
shower
where gnats are blots
of light
that flutter
in the sun.
There are countless constellations!
Hear the sea lions
yowping in the fog!
The drills of life are turning
in each decaying log!

# ANTECHAMBER

*for Larry Littlebird*

# TWO NOTES

The Portuguese Man-o'-war and the Jack Sail-by-the-wind are colonial jellyfish. Each organism is comprised of numbers of specialized individuals reproducing, hunting, and feeding together as a single being.

*Substrate* is the ground or other solid object on which animals move or to which they are attached.

1.

I
KNOW
NOTHING
ABOUT
BOATS.
What I do know
is organisms:
THE
CELLS
and
BEINGS . . .

And I tumble
in the flashy silence

THAT  I  LIGHT  WITH  SELVES

and look for music

WHILE  I  MOIL  UP

around the whirl I make.

This is not a carved wave

or the boundary of a bubble

nor even, sweetly, is it
a Jack Sail-by-the-wind
or Portuguese Man-o'-war.

(I mean those colonial beings,
Medusae clusters
in all their beauty.

We're like them too.

They're us!)

                    Some say
                  we're every thing.

                              Whatever that means . . .

CERTAINLY  WE'RE  DARK  FLESH  MUSIC
       LAYING  OUT  A  SHAPE

                  with Luck
                for outrigger
            and our brain for keel.

—————————————————————

                     DO
                    YOU
                   KNOW
                    WE
                 CROWDED
              ON  THE  LAND?

DO  YOU  KNOW  WE  CROWDED  ON  THE  LAND

                        (The black shapes in pansies
                          are imitating flocks
                        of nectar-drinking flies)

      —around the complex

complex brilliance

of our feedback?

AND
WE
BROKE
THE  SUBSTRATE

and made

the shattered substrate

and made

the substrate shattered.

The forests
and the chaparral

are burned
and grazed
and fenced

in imitation

of our selves.

And now a new
holistic style

is the secret desire

in the strongest

smile.

27

We wish

to lure
perceptions
that make
our being

together
into constellations

like patterns in jade

and waves of stars

that sail through
black velvet

BUT

we're crumpled creatures

that move in helixes

and hurl out

strong

and hungry

loves.

---

WE'RE
RAINBOW-COLORED
KNIGHTS
IN SPASTIC BOATS

28

## UPON A WHIRL-
## POOL.

Each system

                                 that we build

        dissolves itself

                confutes
                its being

                            in its
                      completion.

              Each heiress
            that we kidnap

                    brings

her father's army

              on

                              our heels.

            Surely

                        it is
                      time

to think
this out

           and put

                  the wings,

the pearl encrusted
wings, with
faces on each
feather

and wings upon

each face

on every feather

on our brow.

We
are

OPALS

AND  BLACK  SILHOUETTES
OF  BUFFALOS

and laughing

aching

galaxies

of meat

and breath
and life

bypassing

death

30

in the rippling
           of


                      an


                      aeon.

--------------------------------------

              THIS  BOOK  IS  FAIRY  STUFF.
                      It has

a radiance


                 and trembles real


        in sheens
        of light.


                                          The hands
                                          that wrote
                                          it hang
                                          in space


              as shining freckled
                  APPLES


        in the boughs


                           of time


              where the breeze
                 of luck


is plucking


                      at the trunk.

31

WE'RE

INSTRUMENTS

THAT

PLAY

ourselves.

"What  weapon
has the lion
but himself?"
asks

Keats.

AND
OH

within the cloud
of what there is
we're just as free.

FLESH

plays itself

and states

that it is meat,

*viande,*
and flesh
and
free

32

for
being
selves
if spoken to
in the language

that it understands.

WORDS
&
groans

like vertebrae

are real.

Every thing
at all times

is on the verge

of
liberation;

MUSCLES

crackle

when they loosen.

---

WE'RE
RAINBOW-COLORED
KNIGHTS
IN SPASTIC BOATS

## UPON A WHIRL-POOL.

We're
chunks
of opal
carved from ivory.

We're jellyfish

reflecting

light

in choppy
sunny
seas.

Tendrils
hang
down
from
us
and
stun
and
grasp
a
fish.

Sing Love! Ho Love!
It has lasted
a billion years.

Hey nonny!

Alladay!

Alladay down!

        Away with the frown

    and up

              with the eyelids.

———————————————

WHEN
WE
PLACE
THE
VELVET
SADDLE  BLANKETS
ON
OUR
SELVES
AND
SMILING
lie down to sleep
too often

and grow crazed

            with laziness

    we do not see

       in truth

          it's fear

    that pulls us back

and makes us drowsy

AND  REMOVES  US

FROM  THE  FRONTIER.

For
what

we
touch

is shattered

and all

a-whirl and that's
the way
it is.

WHEN  NECKS  HUNCH
and shoulders turn
to armor

we're like dogs
and cattle

in our kennels

and corrals

BUT
THE  WASH
AND  CHOP
is like

it always was.

                                        WE  CAN
                                          SWIM
                                          in it

                    WE
                    CAN

                    STRETCH
                    AND

                    SING
                    AND

                    WALK
                    LIKE

                    FREE
                    MAMMALS

or an eagle.

                                   The pulse
                                     is all
                                   around,

          the only problem

                    is that it's in

                                        our image.

                    The shattered substrate

imitates the shape

of our

primordial behavior.

WE'RE  BEAUTIFUL!

We built

too well

too definite regarding

what we think

we
are.

There's need for
MUSCULAR  IMAGINATION,
need
for

muscular imagination,

in our motions

not just

imaginary
minds

and magnificent

and constricting

38

but natural

models.

I
AM
A MAMMAL
PATRIOT.

---

I
AM

A MAMMAL
PATRIOT

and LOVE

all life

FOR
LIKE

all life

I
move

in an expanding
helix

through the waves
and fields
and forces

39

when

they're choppy

when

they're sleek
and soft:

it
is
all
the
same
for
it
is me.
I AM MY HAPPY

PAINFUL

body.

Whether cool or hot

I

am

thought.

_____

WE ARE THE
ELECTRICITY

40

AND PADS
OF MATTER

AND
ALL

THE
SUBTLE

BILLIONIC
FIELDS

within
the
cataract
that
twists

through space.

WE
are
the whirlpool
and the jellyfish
and galaxy
and ape

of all our selves

inventing shapes.

We are baby lives
until we die
—locked
within some space—
until

41

some system wraps
itself around
our turning, twisting
motion
and tells us through
the limitations
that we are tied.

BUT still we know
that all conceptions

of boundaries

are
lies.

BUT still we know
that all conceptions

of boundaries

are
lies

and black flocks
of nectar-drinking
flies
are supping

at the yellow pansy's

cup,

are supping

                at the

                                        cup,
            AND

            ALL

        THE  GNATS
        AT  SUNDOWN

    in the rosy
    lovely light

                are

            COUSIN
            ANGELS

            catching
            light

upon their wings

            in the antechamber

                        of the night.

        ———————————————

            WE
            ARE
            MOVING
        SIZELESS  ROOMS
            THAT
            PUSH
            AWAY

                43

THE
DARK.

We're protoplasm

and

we're forests

made

of

sun
and air.

We're broken geodes filled with roses,
vats of honey in the depths of caves,
smiles of squirrels among the maple leaves,
moans of hungry dove babes,
red starfish imagining the waves,
cold
fingers
writing on warm sheets.
We're
white tigers

stalking

endless night.

We're all the loops

of selves

and ghostly elves

44

and trolls and giants

hurling
out

our
fronds

of
luck.

We're all
the energy

we drink
and chew

and suck
from sizelessness

to make

these behemoth

rooms,

to make

these behemoth

rooms.

———————————

JOIN
ME
HERE

45

IN
THIS
SPACE

THAT WE

INVENT

FROM REAL STUFF

WHERE
WE

HAVE
NEVER

laughed, nor danced

nor

sung
before.

WE'RE
RAINBOW-COLORED
KNIGHTS
IN SPASTIC BOATS
UPON A WHIRL-
POOL.

I
AM

A MAMMAL
PATRIOT.

You know

　　　　that we

　　　　　　can walk.

　　　YOU
　　　KNOW

each challenge

　　　　issues

　　　　　　　　from
　　　　　　　　our
　　　　　　　　core.

　　　We've

been
everywhere

　　　　　　　　before.

　　　We're
　　　physiques

of thoughts

　　　　　　　upon a crowded
　　　　　　　land,

　　and all the airiness
　　and aureoles
　　that we create

47

                    are
                    US

            and all the airiness

and aureoles

                                that we create

            are

                                US.

                    WE
                    ARE
                    MOVING
                    SIZELESS
                    ROOMS
                    THAT
                    PUSH
                    AWAY
                    THE
                    DARK

                    AND
                    all

                    the gnats
                    at sundown

        in the rosy
        lovely light

                    are

COUSIN
ANGELS

catching
light

upon their wings

in the antechamber

of the night.

**2.**

WE
ARE
BABY
LIVES
UNTIL
WE DIE.
WE ARE
LOCKED
WITHIN SOME SPACE
UNTIL

A SYSTEM WRAPS

itself around

our turning
twisting
motion.

Then we know
through
limitations
that we
are tied

that we have died.

And yet we're FREE!

We're NEW!

WE'RE BORN
into an entropy!

We'll curl again
from a trigger
of our self.

(A shard of Luck
that's left
behind
starts this beginning

          and we make

                     new shapes

in space.)

      WE  MAKE  NEW  SHAPES  IN  SPACE
      —like a pine cone in the teeth of Time
        or a golden, blinding, rising sun
         reflected in a falcon's eye
        or black pollywogs with spotted
          turgid bellies waking
        in the new-warmed pool

         —WAKING

                  in the new-warmed

pool
          that

          we

         make warm

         our selves.

---

MY MASKS ARE NOT MY SELVES

NO MATTER

HOW THEY RUSH

TO ME.

I'll have
an infinity
of visages

AND

MY
BODY

FEELINGS
ARE

AN
OCEAN

in which float

all realms

and all

dimensions.

I'm a perfect-stepping

raccoon

on a city

52

doorstep;

I'm
a
white
truck

smashing

through

the night.

I'M THE FATHER AND THE MOTHER
OF MY TENSIONS
AND MY LIBERATIONS.

I'M
THE DOORWAY

FOR THE SELVES

that circle

'round

this site.

I'M THE CLUMP OF YELLOW
PANSIES

on the Springtime

cliff.

I'M
THE DOORWAY

53

FOR  THE  SELVES

that circle

'round

this site.

———————————————

AND
ALL
THE  MASKS
THAT  RUSH
TO  ME
TO  STICK

UPON  MY  BROW

are

NOT

my selves.
The system

that we are

uncurls

in every nutrient.

We are reborn
from triggers of the Luck
that we set spinning
into any space we see
or touch, invent,

54

or find

by our

demand.

## THE SILVER CLOUDS OF APRIL ARE A NOISE I HEAR.

The tendrils

are a world

unfurled

upon
the spot
their
absence
once
inhabited

and they crush
or re-create us.

THEN WE ARE NEW.

I have more death

—or I am more FREE.
I am smashed with weight
and motionless
or I can be
an estate of pain
or a billion butterflies
in a dart of glee

                              —OR

                             BOTH

                              AT

                            ONCE

                              IN
                          IMITATION

              of

                      our selves,

                  OR  ALL  AT  ONCE

                              IN
                          IMITATION

          of

                      our selves.

─────────────────────────────────────

        AS  DARK  BLUE

                    AND  PINK

                                        OF  SKIES

    REFLECTED  IN  AN  EVENING  MUDFLAT

          show the shadow

                      of a kingfisher

                                  flashing in

                              56

the mirrored ripples,

or as two dark eyes
stare across
a table
and for an instant
you forget
the thing
you are,
or as
a
YELLOW PANSY

when you discover

you are
A MAMMAL
PATRIOT.

These things

also are
the substrate

and the
chop

and
moil

of what we
swirl in.

NEW MADE SPACES
are as real as dreams

and faces.

57

The consequence of
each act is pure
intensity

BUT

THE
FIELDS

WE
SEE

are not
real

and the ones
we do not
see
are
as
real
as
anything

that is.

Where dark flies
are supping
at the cup,

we move in helixes

newborn

as

fields.

58

AND
ALL

THESE
THOUGHTS

ARE
DREAMS

AND
BEAMS

OF
SPEED

AND
BREATH

(AND
BREADTH

AND
BREAD

AND
DEATH)

AND
SLOWNESS

moving

LIGHTNING
FAST

TO
FORMULATE

A
WORLD

OF

SINGING
NEURONS

IN

THE
CHOIR

OF
SNOW

AND
STONE

AND
CYCLONES

MELTING
INTO

MEN
AND

SPINNING
CLOUDS

OF
MEAT

60

　　　　　　　　　　　　—SPINNING
　　　　　　　　　　　　CLOUDS

　　　　　　　　　　　OF
　　　　　　　　　　　MEAT

　　　projecting

　　　　　　　　organisms

　　　　　　　　　　　　　　and not ships

　　or boats,

　　　　　　　　but melting

　　　　　　　　　　　things

　　　　that take
　　　　the shapes

　　　　　　　　of skulls

　　　　　　　　　　　　　and
　　　　　　　　　　　　　fins

and tentacles
and throats,

　　　　　　　　but melting

　　　　　　　　　　　　things

　　　　that take
　　　　the shapes

of skulls

and
fins

and tentacles
and throats

in these behemoth rooms.

---

THE  FACE
IS  MANY
COLORS,
MANY
PATCHES,
AREAS
OF
LUMINOSITIES

that melt

into

the shoulders.

The consequence

of

each act

is sheer
intensity.

THE BODY

flows
upward

from the substrate

the shattered substrate
incorporating

chop
and moil

into

the shape and structure.

The waves
ARE
US.

The generation

of our being

makes

the light
and

color

AND
WE
ENGULF

our

ends

and our beginnings

in

this

floating

rolling

waving

breaking

shaking

gliding.

We are

the flare

of light

from gnat's wings

in

the sundown

and
all

64

the
radiance
of
stars.

I
AM

A MAMMAL
PATRIOT

I AM!

I AM!

I AM!

---

THE GESTURE
THAT
WE MAKE
INITIATES
THE
SYSTEM.

It brings

the whirlpool

to the eagle

in the universe

of thoughtless

thinking
waves.

65

The organism
is the ship
that hurls us
through the state
across the chasm
we

create.

We're infinities of wings
and stings

and bites

and kisses

and of loops.

The world we make of light
is April
AND

an

instant

is

the frontier.

We're storms
of thunder

and jellyfish

and sloops

66

and blooming
things

upon
the substrate.

Sing alladay

alladay down

away with the frown

and up

with the eyelids!

Sing Love! Ho Love!
It has lasted

a billion years.

———————————

"WHO  WILL  GET  A  CURING
IN  THE
TOTAL
COSMOS?
WHO  WILL  GET  A  CURING?"
The
SHAMAN
is dressed
in clown flesh
clothing.
The doctor
is as transient
as his meat.

Any object

is the frontier

and also is our style.
Our
consciousness
is an aggregate of particles
and
facets
and dimensions
that comment

on themselves.

We are waves

and forces intertwined

in invisible totality.

We are the very selves

we flee

from in our shade

of death.

WE ARE THE BRILLIANT-BEAMING
GOLDEN-SMILING GODHEAD
OF THE ROSY GNAT'S WING

and the trampling

of a living mastodon

as we take

each breath.

Everything is mist that curls
in smoke above the cabin
after snowfall,
and chunks of turquoise,
fur of chinchillas,
barks of wolf cubs,
scarlet bridges looming
in the rainstorm,
warm cars driving through
the night,
purple spiny sea urchins lodged
in sea-beaten crevices,
songs of matter that the stars sing,
patterned quilts with flower faces
sewn by grandmas  .  .  .

WE  ARE  ALL

—ALL—

THE  SELVES  WE  BRING

to circle

round

this site!

_____

WE'RE
BEAUTIFUL
WE

69

ARE
THE ANCIENT,

NEWBORN

perfect

stuff!

WE
ONLY

shape

our state
too well

in

imitation

of

our selves.

You and I are HEROES
of our future particles.

We're otters

swimming

in

70

the shadows
of

the now.

_____

YOU
KNOW

each challenge

issues

from
our
core.

We've

been
everywhere

before.

We're
physiques

of thoughts

upon a crowded
land,

and all the airiness
and aureoles
that we create

71

are
US

and all the airiness
and aureoles

that we create

are

US.

WE
ARE
MOVING
SIZELESS
ROOMS
THAT
PUSH
AWAY
THE
DARK

AND
all

the gnats
at sundown

in the rosy
lovely light

are

COUSIN
ANGELS

72

CATCHING
LIGHT

UPON  THEIR  WINGS

in the antechamber

of the night.

# SESTINA

WE ARE WHITE FLAMES IN BLACK
and we are silver candles,
smiles on roses,
newborn babes,
otter consciousness,
and night shades.

We are ghostly shades
and the shapes of black
bonfires that melt through consciousness.
Perceptions are candles
and we are babes
who imagine the thorns of roses.

The petals of roses
make pink and blue shades
and scents over babes
who fear no black
candles
in the hugeness of consciousness.

We are the autumn of consciousness
giving birth to spring roses
by the silverware next to the candles.
Not all of the shades
nor all of the purple and black
convinces us we are other than babes.

You know we are babes.
Each thing is our consciousness.
The cave is black
but it is filled with roses
—and though we draw the shades
we light the candles.

The bright glow is from the candles
in the hands of babes
who outline the shades
of perception in consciousness.
See there are roses!
They stand in the black.

Those are candles of consciousness
that show we are babes and floating roses.
We are shades of flesh turning on black.

## ABOVE SAN FRANCISCO

—THE LIGHTS OF THE CITY
BETWEEN
GRAY-BLACK CLOUDS,
the scent
of chocolate,
the aura
of murderous
movies, the moors
of Northern California,
and mysterious girls.
See, the banner of samsara
unfurls!

# FRAGMENT

*for Baker-roshi*

AH
YES,

how perfect
to be within a dream

inside
a body

in a
VISION!

How
REAL!

HOW  SOLID!

I
am
the
body
!

The dream
is flesh!

APPEARANCE
is my breath!

76

I
AM
THE
HUMMINGBIRD

OF
CHANCE
!

# SONG FROM A PLAY

—TITANS BREATHING IN THE ROSE,
the velvet touch where beauty flows,
the pansy's lip upon the moss,
all
free us,
free us
from what is dross.
The cosmic cards are more than chance.
The world is shaped within
a glance,
where beauty flows,
where beauty flows
when duty glows  . . .


# A DEVOTION

AT ROOT LET ME BE
AS BLIND, AMORAL,
ETERNALLY
HUNGRY
as
creatures
afloat like living
opals in a wave-crashed
sea.

# SCARLET KNIGHT

POLITICS STARTS WITH THE BARREL
OF A GUN,
says the great
dead one.
Red is the answer to all
—as is white.
We are the heroes of our problems
and the ends of all delight.
Ah,
kiss him quick!
Blood pours out the window.
Hello to the starry heavens!
Goodbye
to the final fight!
Hail
Chairman
Mao,
poet and scarlet knight!

# THIS  LIGHT

LIKE  A  VULTURE'S  FLIGHT,  MY  HEART
which is a mind, beats out
and floats
and fills the resonance of space
with its extension of my face
and toes and hair
in sound
that's made
by
pulse
of
blood.
Ha!
Oh!
Ah!
—it goes!

The sun-cup
in the sunny, dewy
meadow
reflects back the touch
of bright in the raptor's eye.
The songs we sing are no more
nor less than the deer mouse
cry!


2.


This light—these plaster walls—
are both my skin,
like histories,
like sighs!

80

I
am
every
place

at once.

My
mind
grows thin

and
I

begin

to be

the solid

bulk

of consciousness,

the final self

I start

to realize.

# HEARTACHE PAIN

HEARTACHE PAIN IS NO SMALL MATTER.
When we love we scatter
all our stuff and all our selves

past

the place

the farthest reach

of net
can gather.

Then our golden daydreams
flash to attack
pulsars. We speak

like scarlet macaws

of our numbness

and stumble

like puppets

on

rubber

strings!

I say

let us

talk
clear

AND  BE  THE  TITANS
that we know

we
are.

Even bearing this gray hair
I'll always be
a brown-eyed boy!

Your touch

of hands

shall ever
be

my joy!

# SENTIMENTAL PEACE

THE QUANTUM MECHANICS
OF BLACK HOLES,
the dreams of mink,
chinchilla stoles,
the taste of Scotch
upon the rocks,
the flocks of cormorants
upon the piles,
silhouettes of profiles
from long dead men,
even pressed violets
and the passing thought
of
a
long-gone
friend
—ALL
THESE

like
space

and
time

and
mounds

of round

black stones

are
real.

We are each feeling

that we kiss or steal!


# ACCURSED WITH NORMALITY

ACCURSED WITH NORMALITY
despite your beauty

you'll live and die

like many others.

What minor tragedy

will push
you past

the brink?

You'll kiss your Fate

on his swart lips
while he hugs you

and you slip
to nothingness with
faintest scent
of plainest breath

still drifting

in the backstage
of mortality.

Among the benches,
curled wigs,
and painted skies
—your
piquant hopes
are

lies.

All pleasantness dissolves
to dust.

•

Even an iron hammer
changes into rust.

## WRITTEN ON THE FLYLEAF
## OF ASHVAGOSHA'S
### *THE AWAKENING OF FAITH*


PERFECT ENLIGHTENMENT,
I kneel and pray
to your bright hand and your chin
asking for sugar. Oh, sorrowless state,
happy black face.
Oh, lap-full of pearls  . . .
Pillows of eternal green velvet  . . .
Formation of nests in continents of sound  . . .
Still drapes in the hurricane  . . .
Snuffed candle becoming coolness  . . .
Tricycles lighted by the glare of sirens  . . .
Thou art the better of thyself
here already
and I yearn to make it
to
thee.


1963–1977

# FOR JOANNA

HOW BEAUTIFUL GRAVITY IS!
Can it get one high?
My
heart
is
a
sky

full
of

clouds

of blood

when

I run.

I grow
wise and
young

till

I

die.

# INDEX
# OF TITLES
# AND FIRST LINES